THE STONE WALLS

OF IRELAND

THE STONE WALLS OF IRELAND

ALEN MacWEENEY
AND
RICHARD CONNIFF

WITH 110 COLOUR ILLUSTRATIONS

Thames and Hudson

PAGE 1: *a walled lane on Inishmaan.*

PAGES 2–3: *in County Clare, a wall made of Liscannor flags.*

PAGES 4–5: *the hounds of the County Galway Hunt.*

PAGES 6 AND RIGHT: *late afternoon in County Clare.*

CONTENTS

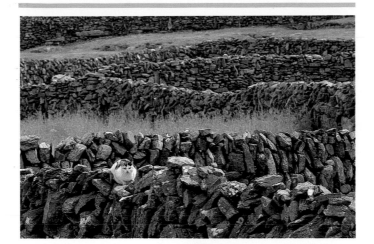

INTRO-
DUCTION

THE WEATHER
that Sunday was so fine it would have made
a cat laugh. The temperature pushed into the
upper seventies toward noon, and, with a
thirst coming on, I slipped into a smoky pub
near St. Brigid's Well in Liscannor for a pint.
A gregarious, salmon-skinned man who had

PRECEDING PAGES
An uncleared landscape in County Kerry (page 10);
the walled-up world of Inisheer, the Aran Islands.

obviously had the same idea, only earlier, was soon inquiring what had brought me to Ireland. "Is it roots?" he asked, sizing me up instantly as an American.

"Stone walls," I replied, and was pleased to see him momentarily baffled. The walls, I explained, were everywhere in Ireland. ("Well, I suppose they are," he said.) Indeed, they were the dominant feature of the Irish landscape ("They may be," he conceded, having opened this Pandora's box), and a scholar in Dublin had declared that "the care and effort that went into them would have built the pyramids of Egypt a hundred times over." ("Well, now.") I had an idea that the preference for building walls rather than pyramids said a good deal about the ways the Irish people have come to live with the land and with each other. The drinker concluded, I think, that I was a bit mad.

The proposition that I had put before him was, admittedly, an odd one: that you could see a country not just through its literature, or its great monuments, or its people, but through its walls. It suggested an oblique, not to say opaque, point of view.

On the other hand, it was a proposition that made perfect sense if you stood on Croagh Patrick, the mountain of St. Patrick, and looked north to the far side of Clew Bay, where stone walls break up the sloping fields into a sun-dappled patchwork. It made sense, too, if you looked down from one of the heights of the Bloody Foreland in County Donegal: the small lowland fields there are all divided and subdivided by ancient, irregular walls into tiny triangles, ovals, indefinable snippets of land, too small for any practical purpose, that nonetheless enclose hand-tied oat ricks or a cow with

OVERLEAF
*A slope below the ancient fort of Dun Eochla on
Inishmore, the Aran Islands.*

its haunches turned to the lashing, white Atlantic. It made sense, too, on Inisheer, one of the Aran Islands, where there are no trees or shrubs to mar the horizon, but only endless lovely walls, more intricate and numerous than the crazing on a glazed pot, enclosing, for the most part, nothing. It made sense, in fact, almost anywhere out of doors in Ireland. According to one estimate, there are 240,000 miles of field walls in Ireland—more than in any other country. The walls are the primary, inescapable fact of one of the most admired landscapes in the world.

Who built these walls, and when? What were they fencing in or fencing out? How did mere muscle move the great boulders in this wall, or accumulate the fortresslike mass of that one? Why would someone have created a walled-in field with no apparent gate—indeed, a vast honeycomb of such fields, with not even a roadway or footpath for access? Every visitor to Ireland asks these questions, or others like them.

The Irish themselves ask such questions, sometimes disparagingly. "A man from Tipperary came through," a wall-builder on Inisheer told me, "and he said, 'Why don't you knock down the walls and get rid of the small fields?' And I said, 'What would we do with the stones?' He said, 'Put them in a heap.' People say all kinds of things." The answers are sometimes mildly derisive. When Americans ask how he gets his livestock into a field with no gates, the same wall-builder customarily replies, "We have a helicopter." Or he might gesture at a 1,200-pound cow and declare, "I lift her over." Still, it makes sense to inquire about the walls. Farmers have formed these walls into the spine and the ribs of

the Irish landscape, and the shaping of a landscape in any country is one of the great human endeavors.

René Dubos described the gradual remaking of the world, from wilderness into "humanized" rural countryside, as "the wooing of earth." He borrowed the phrase from the Bengali poet Rabindranath Tagore for whom the shaping of the European continent by human labor constituted the "heroic love-adventure of the West, the active wooing of the earth."

An Irish farmer would perhaps laugh at the phrase: he is more often cursing the hardscrabble earth than wooing it. But the walls say otherwise; they suggest a long and patient seduction of the land to the purposes of agriculture. On Inisheer, there is a patch at the back of the island that remains in its natural state. It is a rubble heap, strewn with boulders on a fissured bed of limestone. It is utterly barren. Indeed, only where farmers have drawn back the boulders, formed them into walls to break the sea wind, and carted sand, seaweed, and manure to manufacture soil on the limestone surface does anything like an environment begin to appear. The making of this strange, walled-up island world was very much a "heroic love adventure," a wooing and treasuring up of earth. One cannot but wonder how many generations of labor went into the effort, and what toll it took on the spirit of the islanders.

People do not change the land without the land in turn changing them. Dubos speculated, for instance, that the deforestation of ancient Greece might have indirectly fostered the flowering of logic: "I have wondered whether the dark and ferocious divinities of the preclassical Greek period

A walled lane through the Burren, County Clare.

did not become more serene and more playful precisely because they had emerged from the dark forests into the open landscape. Would logic have flourished if Greece had remained covered with an opaque tangle of trees?"

No one would suggest that anything like logic resulted from the remaking of the Irish landscape (including its nearly total deforestation). But I wanted to know what *had* resulted. Or rather, having lived with the Irish temperament—often charming, at other times ferocious, drunk with language and yet emotionally constricted, both individualistic and socially timid, joyously combative, and endlessly, sometimes bitterly, quarrelsome—I wondered what part the landscape and the walls had had in forming it. E. Estyn Evans, the Irish folklorist, once wrote: "The history of rural Ireland could be read out of doors, had we the skill, from the scrawling made by men in the field boundaries of successive periods." One could read not just the history, I thought, but perhaps also the soul of rural Ireland. In the walls, Evans said, "the unlettered countryman wrote his runes on the land. . . ."

TALKING POINTS

THE WALLS look as though they have been there forever: mottled with lichen and bearded with moss; woven together with vines, hedges, and trees; running, in more than one place, straight across a shallow stream bed, as if the wall were there before the water; emerging, in

other places, from the low tide mark, as if the walls splashed ashore with the first settlers in Ireland, 8,000 years ago.

"All the people are dead now who was building walls," a man known locally as the Kaiser assured me one afternoon in County Kerry. It was the sort of remark you heard everywhere in Ireland: the walls were built "centuries ago, I suppose." Even "thousands and thousands of years ago." Or "in olden times." And what did he himself do for a living, I asked the Kaiser. Well, he built walls.

Long ago, of course? Not at all, he said. There was the one in Ballyferriter, built a year or two ago to "close up" around a man's house, and another outside the church. There was a fine new wall across from the pub in Ventry. There was the wall he was going to be building soon around Paudy O'Shea's new pub. And of course there was Sean Moran's wall on the Conor Pass Road in Dingle—I must've heard about it—a wall of such magnificence that people stopped their cars dead in the middle of the road to admire it: "You'd *have* to stop to look at it," he said, as if to explain away their poor driving habits. "You'd be blind if you didn't." He would show it to me himself, in fact.

The following Saturday, as arranged, we headed off around the tip of the Dingle Peninsula, stopping at a number of places not listed in *The Kerry Guide,* including Sean Moran's wall—a structure of double thickness, 6 feet in height, around a field where sheep grazed. "The best wall around, I'd say, in Kerry," the Kaiser ventured, on his own craftsmanship. "There are no sheep going to be coming out of there soon. Or cattle."

Beehive huts and stone ricks on the Dingle Peninsula.

As we drove, he talked about his craft. The common stone in the area was red sandstone, which breaks away in relatively flat tablets well suited to construction. "There's a bed for every one," the Kaiser explained. "You put it there and say, 'Get in it.'" It was sound material for a wall like, well, Sean Moran's. He'd set the stones there so snugly, he said, that "you couldn't pass a blade of grass across it with a pliers. Sean Moran'll be dead and rotting before it falls down. You'd travel a long time before you saw the likes of that again. You'd travel all Ireland, I suppose."

He lamented the tendency to use barbed wire and electric fencing, which give no shelter for the crops or the animals. Some farmers even bulldozed stone walls to make bigger fields. Sean Moran, of course, would need no wiring. One local man so admired the towering wall at Moran's place that he went out every day with his dog and gazed at it for a half-hour at a time, until one day the dog (gone mad with boredom) got away from him and was killed (doubtless by a driver who was looking at the wall instead of the road). "A lot of people came out to look at it when it was built. Thousands of people. All Dingle came." The wall achieved its rightful status as a conversation piece; it became that estimable thing in Irish country life—a "talking point." For its builder, anyway.

The Kaiser complained about a local farmer who wanted a wall built. "He told me, 'My cattle don't wear glasses looking at the wall. I don't want no fancy work.' The man had red trousers on and a white jacket and he only wanted a plain wall. 'Something thrown up. No fancy work.' And then he put in this big white stone that looks like the arse of a tank in there." Sean Moran's wall, by contrast,

At Slea Head, farther out on the peninsula, walls still break the sea wind, and old stone cottages serve as shelter for livestock.

was a subtle masterpiece. "You don't see the likes of that in Connemara, do you? You'd travel the world. 'Tis a job forever and ever. And no cement."

Any comparison with Sean Moran's wall is of course invidious, but in that regard it was like a number of others we passed that day on the Dingle Peninsula: dry stone walls, built "forever and ever," of a sort that would make even a modern wall-builder think the craft was one practiced mostly long ago, in days gone by. At the end of the peninsula, for instance, the ancient fort of Dunbeg walls off a small promontory from attack by land. The final line of defense is a massive stone barrier stepped up on the inside with walkways for men fighting with their backs to the Atlantic. No one really knows who built it, or against what foe. Farther on toward Slea Head, the slopes are dotted with beehive huts, monastic dwellings huddled together within small stone circles built high to shut out the world. Around the forts and these anchoritic retreats, the land is of a sort to keep monks and other farmers thin. But it is also well walled, and the field walls, too, look as if they have been there forever. Some of them are sod and stone. The grass grows sideways on them, and they look like yard-high ridges — elongated fins — of lawn. Elsewhere the walls are densely packed piles of flat sandstone. They run up to the mountaintops, enclosing fields pitched at an angle of 30 degrees. The scenery, out to the Blasket Islands, is spectacular, but it's the slope that takes your breath away.

If these walls appear ancient, it may be with good reason. A few Irish walls are as modern as Sean Moran's, and many are of far more recent vintage than a passer-by would surmise. But archeologists

Patrick Coll and neighbors on the way to a bus for
Sunday Mass in Gorthahork, County Donegal.

have established that the building of walls in Ireland goes back to the Neolithic Age. They have found walls running *underneath* a prehistoric burial cairn in County Down. There, and all along the coast from Kerry to Antrim, farmers cutting turf have stumbled onto field walls—whole systems of walls, in some cases—hidden for millennia by the peat blanket. These subterranean walls run, in one case, from the waterline to a point 600 feet above sea level. At another site, the buried farm has much the shape of a modern one, with half-acre tillage plots, fields of 3 or 4 acres, and a long straight fence more than a mile long, apparently separating one family's holdings from another's. The blanket peat that hid these old fields began to build up around 1000 B.C., as a result of early land clearing and deforestation. The walls beneath this blanket are thus probably 3,000 to 4,000 years old and are compounded of stone and sod, in the same manner as walls built on the present surface within the last century. In some places, the old walls emerge from the turf and continue on the surface as present-day boundaries. Like modern countrymen, prehistoric farmers doubtless cast a cool, appraising eye on one another's fields from across such walls.

But while the Irish landscape abounds in prehistoric and Early Christian antiquities, the walls generally do not date back that far, and the sense of continuity between modern walls and those of prehistoric farmers is an illusion. Most walls in Ireland went up no earlier than the agricultural revolution. The network of walls and hedges that we think of as timelessly defining the Irish countryside was, in fact, cast over the landscape like a web beginning in about 1750. Before that, much, if not

*In the background, a wall affords some protection to a
stack of turf, which will be used as fuel.*

most, of Ireland was, in effect, a great unfenced cow pasture. "Their fields lie open and unclosed," declared *Advertisements for Ireland* in 1623. Where proper fields existed, an anonymous writer added a few years later, they were "no better fenced than a midwife's toothless gums." In Donegal, in the middle of the nineteenth century, a landlord declared: "We suppose it would not be believed that in this district, until very lately, fences were altogether unknown."

Indeed, the Irish seem to have had something close to a split personality on the subject of walls. Scattered across the landscape by their pastoral, cattle-herding way of life, with nothing like the security of a town or village nearby, early Irish farmers commonly walled themselves in. The strongest farmers put up their houses within raths or ring-forts, a form associated with Celtic settlers of the first millennium A.D. Thirty thousand of these raths survive around Ireland, visible, in the words of a Kerry farmer, as "old roundish rings of mouldy stone and sods." These grassy corrugations in the earth are all that remain even of Tara, once the seat of power over much of Ireland.

The raths are so well preserved partly because grazing was always more important in Ireland than the plow, but also because farmers regarded the raths as "fairy forts" and would not touch them. In Ulster in 1958, for example, a Land Commission work crew was building a fence in the course of rearranging land holdings in a congested district. "But an ancient rath lay in the path of the fence," a local newspaper reported. "The workmen refused to dig holes in the rath. They said they would die soon if they lifted a sod. A Land Commission supervisor suggested that two of the oldest men in the

A horse seeks shelter as rain whips in off the north Donegal coast.

RIGHT

A County Donegal farmer, John McClein, at his gate near Raphoe.

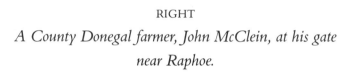

locality might have no fear of death. Two men, one of 97, the other 95, were asked and indignantly refused. They said that life was 'as sweet as the fairy music they often heard from the rath.'" Such caution has given the Irish landscape the quality of a palimpsest, with the earthworks of earlier civilizations still visible in the modern fields. But that is changing. Unfearing bulldozers now frequently level raths, and at Tara the raths sometimes serve as a sort of makeshift dirt bike course. Carrot-haired boys on fat-wheeled bicycles rise and disappear over the humpy landscape as if pedaling over waves.

The raths were once a place for a farmer to drive his livestock, to protect his wealth from hit-and-run cattle raiders. What field walls existed seem mostly to have been huddled around these refuges and around monastic sites. They formed the tillage plots of the "infield." But beyond them, in the "outfield," Irish farmers seem to have felt something like an abhorrence for walls. The occasional crop planted in a portion of the outfield would necessarily be enclosed, to keep the animals from trampling it. But the enclosure would be wicker, with stakes driven into the ground and rods woven around them. When the crop came in, the fence came down. The rods served as fuel in winter, and the outfield survived as open range.

The transition to the enclosed landscape was abrupt and painful, entailing the destruction of the pastoral way of life. If the walls do not figure much in Irish folklore, the lingering sense of loss connected with them may be one important reason. It may seem that the pastoral farmers had little to lose. Irish pastoralism had few outside admirers. Giraldus Cambrensis (the surname means "from

BELOW

In the Mourne, County Down, granite walls define the lives of goats, sheep, geese, and cattle. Locals say weasellike stoats sometimes live in the walls and prey on newborn livestock.

RIGHT

Only sheep thrive in this wild and inhospitable Killarney landscape.

A graveyard at an abandoned abbey in Claregalway.

Wales") complained in about 1200 that the Irish "have not progressed at all from the primitive habits of pastoral living." He also wrote, "They are a wild and inhospitable people. They live on beasts only, and live like beasts." The Irish still quote the phrase, and have not forgiven its author.

Numerous English visitors dwelt with quivering revulsion on such customs as the keeping of cattle inside the house (for safety perhaps, and also as a source of warmth), the storing of dung in heaps outside the door (for manuring the crops), and the tumbling into one bed of numerous naked or ill-clad members of both sexes (here the authors seem to have suffered, behind their nosegays, from a certain voyeuristic fascination). Such accounts, by characterizing the Irish as savages, partly served to justify English usurpation of the land; they were no doubt also partly true. But almost all English visitors particularly misunderstood the central feature of pastoral life—"booleying," the seasonal shifting of cattle from around the dwellings out to remote pasturage. They repeatedly described Irish life as largely nomadic and Irish cultivation of the soil as minimal or nonexistent. It was an understandable mistake. In times of trouble, which were frequent, farmers could retreat into the hills and survive on their livestock. Elizabethan soldiers generously demonstrated this phenomenon for authors who followed in their wake: they dispossessed farmers, routing them into the hills and destroying their crops. The Irish had not been nomads, but that is what some of them perforce became.

As English landlords and settlers took over during the seventeenth century, widespread fencing of the land began almost immediately. Their methods had obvious and impressive advantages. In

Cattle line up at a limestone wall near Loughrea,
County Galway.

County Meath, for example, 5,000 acres of "waste sheep walk" were drained, limed, and fenced off into arable fields of ten acres each, for settlement by French and English Protestants.

These fences were elaborate affairs. An eighteenth-century visitor described them as typically consisting of an earthen embankment between drainage ditches 6 feet wide and 5 feet deep. The bank was usually planted with hedges and with trees for lumber. (In Ireland, for unknown reasons, the word "ditch" came to apply to the raised bank, rather than to the trenches from which it was formed. The word is now used to denote almost any form of raised boundary, including an unmortared—but not a mortared—stone wall; a mortared stone wall is known as a "wall." By the same logic, the word "moat" or "mote" refers in Ireland not to a water-filled trench around a castle, but to the raised and fortified platform enclosed by the trench; it derives from the Norman French word for "mound." The traveler in Ireland must therefore be prepared to hear about people climbing ditches and walking, like Christ, on moats. These are merely lexical differences, not miracles.)

The single most important benefit of enclosing the countryside was that it made the livestock farming for which Ireland was best suited more systematic and productive. Confining the movement of cattle within an enclosed field meant that the grass would be grazed more thoroughly and the manure concentrated in a field that could subsequently be planted with crops. With cattle no longer wandering freely over the open outfield, more land came under cultivation. Crop rotation was possible, along with the use of hay and roots as winter fodder.

Sometimes "the stones do be falling down and you've got to rise them up." Sheep are often to blame.

LEFT

A cliff face near Ballyshannon, County Donegal.

Unfortunately for the Irish, the countryside that was being fenced in had been their common grazing ground. Not only were their ancient ways being supplanted by new and foreign methods; they were themselves being forced out, especially in the fertile lowlands. They responded, in places, by hacking down the landlords' hedges to burn for winter fuel. Later, in the eighteenth century, secret societies like the Ribbonmen vented their anger at a variety of grievances by mutilating the landlords' livestock. In Munster, he Whiteboys burned the alien settlers' crops and leveled walls across former common grazing ground. By then, however, the walls had already wrought a singular, irreversible change in Irish life: they had made the herder obsolete.

By eliminating this central figure in the pastoral tradition, enclosure may have ensured the subsequent dissolution of the Irish language and culture. Estyn Evans, who saw the last holdouts of the booleying system in the middle of the present century, gave a bittersweet account of that way of life. Herding was the child's "first emancipation from his mother's skirts," he wrote — so much so that the Irish word for "boy" was simply *buchaill,* or "herder." It was also the last job of the elderly:

The herders themselves were kept on a short tether, never leaving the cows, and the association of old and young amid the sights and sounds of nature was no doubt the means of passing on knowledge and lore and keeping alive tradition. Both young and old were put out of work when the hedged ditch replaced the bare banks and balks of the open fields. The coming of permanent enclosure must have had many other sociological as well as economic consequences. The physical narrowing of horizons, the obstruction of the distant view, the increased privacy, were surely partly responsible for the decline in natural poetry and in the spirit of communal living which marked the course of the nineteenth century.

But if enclosure ended one way of life, it also began another, drawing out the latent Irish mania for walls. There was, as Evans wrote, a "lingering tradition of wall-building among the stony hills" and, as it revived, the landscape "blossomed with intricate garlands of dry stone walls." The walls entered not just every field, but every life and every aspect of life. They became drying racks, clotheslines, coat hooks, scratching posts, hiding places for poteen, and dumps for weapons. They served as shelter for outdoor classrooms—the so-called hedge schools—when formal education of Catholics was for a time outlawed. The walls were a place for lovers to hide, and also for eavesdroppers. They were instruments of spite and weapons for assault, but they were also children's playthings. (Outside Mullingar, for instance, children running small stones across the resonant coping stones have worn a long groove in a "musical wall"; the groove is generations old, but it is also still fresh.) They were a source of entertainment and of "divilment," which was and is a national sport.

As boundaries, the walls became manifestations of the Irish fondness for small fiefdoms and the gleeful cultivation of petty divisions, but they were at times also instruments of self-destructive

OVERLEAF
Dermot Trainor likes to think the walls he builds on his
farm near Kilkeel, County Down, will still look good in
a thousand years.

generosity by enabling the land to be further and further subdivided. For peasant and landlord alike, the walls were a way of showing wealth, power, craftsmanship. As such, like Sean Moran's wall, they were talking points. They were also objects of delight entirely on their own. If the walls closed off the Irish from certain wilder, more naturalistic feelings, still they had a beauty of their own, to which the Irish were hardly blind. (*Tarry Flynn*, Patrick Kavanagh's novel of country life in County Monaghan, is, for example, shot through with walls and hedges. One moment the excitable protagonist is counting the stones in a wall as an exercise in self-control; the next he is suffused with lyrical feelings: "The snails climbing up the stones of the fences and the rushes and thistles in the meadow beyond seemed to be putting a quilt of peace around his heart.")

Finally, of course, the walls had something to do with the business of farming. They were a place to put stones when the fields were being picked clean. They were a way to mark field boundaries. And they were barriers to keep cattle in the pasturage and donkeys out of the cabbages. Indeed, building good walls quickly became synonymous with sound farming in Ireland. It was something that got into the blood. The story is told of County Galway farmers who had complained all their lives about the miserable land, where stones grew like mushrooms and walls divided farms less into fields than into cubicles. In time, the Land Commission relocated them to the rich, wide fields of County Meath. They complained then, of course, that they hadn't enough stones to build a decent fence. There is a saying, still repeated in parts of Ireland: "You can tell a farmer by his ditches."

THE
NORTH

ONE AFTER-
noon, as I was making my way through
County Donegal, I found myself rounding the
Bloody Foreland, Ireland's northwestern tip,
on foot. The weather had been fair, but it was
suddenly as if I'd strolled into a gale in the
middle of the North Atlantic. Taking shelter
behind a shed, I met a local man and fell into
conversation about the weather in these parts,

*Using crowbars and wooden planks, farmers moved
massive boulders to clear the fields and form the walls of
the Bloody Foreland (both).*

which was changeable. "There's nothing from here till you get to America," he assured me, "so the sea has plenty of room to work up a rage."

The coastline below seemed, indeed, to be waiting out the present battering with routine stoicism. Waves crashed into the rocks and threw up columns of water taller than the nearest cottage. The rain came sideways, in blinding spates. Smoke whipped off a chimney top. A cow in a field the size of a one-car garage took shelter by a wall.

The weather aside, this seemed an unlikely place to make a farm, much less the network of farms stretched out below. Walls broke up the land into patches of bright green on a long plateau just above sea level. "There's nice bits of land inside the ditches," the local man said. But above the road, the land remained as God made it. It was not really land at all, but a hodgepodge of granite boulders, as close together as potatoes in a sack, with some dirt thrown in between as a sort of packing material. Heather, not grass, grew here. It was daunting, even in retrospect, to contemplate how farmers working with their hands changed this gray rubble into the unblemished green of the cleared land. The walls that they'd made from the rough stone had an almost crystalline neatness.

"It was never a place for a human being to live, down there among the rocks," a local historian later explained. "But they were driven out. They were mostly people who were chased out of East Donegal during the Plantation of Ulster." The clearing of the land would thus probably have begun in the decades after 1608, when Scottish and English Protestants supplanted the native Irish on choice land throughout Ulster. Displaced farmers moved to marginal land on hillsides, near bogs, on offshore islands, and all along the rugged west coast. On the Bloody Foreland, they were still clearing land within living memory.

The old people tend to regard those times with a certain admiration, especially when comparing former generations to young people today. "They couldn't do it now. Not the right class of people at all. The young men today wouldn't even lift a stone."

They no longer need to. For a variety of reasons, including tourism, people have grown away from the land. "They've got very modern," said a woman who'd been raised in the area and was herself only back to visit. "They get their milk delivered."

People who work for a living say the dole is now commonplace. Housing grants have littered the countryside with bungalows built in a hurry and often left with an air of disorder and incompletion, out of place in the hand-made landscape of the past. In a foul eatery nearby, a "Light Fantastic" video jukebox plays and the air is heavy with stale grease for fish and chips. Here, where the customers are native speakers of the Irish language, a Dublin-born visitor mutters lines from Yeats: "Scorn the sort now growing up / All out of shape from toe to top." But in the same poem, Yeats also wrote, "Cast your mind on other days / That we in coming times may be / Still the indomitable Irishry." Outside, in every field, the walls serve as a reminder.

"They were happier in those days," a farmer told me. "They had less to eat." The farmer lived in an

LEFT

*John McConnell stands amid the ripe oats on his farm
in Ballymartin, County Down.*

OVERLEAF

*For a makeshift gate, any material will suffice: a wheel
rim, scrap lumber, the hood of a car.*

old-style cottage, and the air inside was blue with the smoke of his turf fire. He was shaving in front of a steaming basin of water on his kitchen table. When a farmer wanted to make a field, he recalled, going back to his own youth, he would bring together a few neighbors, usually in winter, when other farm chores were less pressing. They pried the stones out with crowbars and dragged them to the field boundaries on a plank. Straightforward work, repeated over and over, with crippling, herniating, bone-bending results.

"They had nothing to do then. No lounges, no pubs. So they had to do some work. Times was bad. No money. And they had to take the stones out of the land to make ground for potatoes and to make shelter for the crops they were putting in."

The Plantation pushed back the original Irish inhabitants of Ulster onto just 10 percent of the land, though they continued to be tolerated outside marginal areas as tenants and laborers. The Irish were not just relegated to the less desirable land, but they also had to pay twice the rent the new settlers paid. The memory of "hard rates" persists, though the landlord system died a century ago. The farmer had to make his tiny holding feed the family and pay the rent, and it took a delicate balance to avoid the extremes of starvation or eviction. These pressures, combined with steady population growth, produced the characteristic Irish malady: "land hunger." And the only cure for land hunger was to make new fields.

"Every year they did a bit," the farmer said, as his shaving water cooled. "It was all manpower that

A Union Jack flies over a modern housing development just outside Londonderry's seventeenth-century city wall.

PRECEDING PAGES
An ancient god and a modern sentry post at Bishop's Gate in Londonderry.

put the walls up. They were very strong, the men going. That stuff must've been very good they were eating. No hamburgers, no fancy bread, no cakes. Those walls were put up by baking bread made in the fire, like that." He indicated his hearth. "And oaten bread, and potatoes and fresh herrings. The food must've been very good, what there was of it. They weren't drinking Coca-Cola in those days."

ACROSS DONEGAL AND OVER THE BORDER INTO what is now Northern Ireland, the same historical events produced a wholly different type of wall. Atop an old monastic site on a hill between Lough Swilly and Lough Foyle, the leaders of the Ulster Plantation made their headquarters in the walled city of Londonderry. The wall survives. Built in 1617 at a cost of £8,357, it remains a formidable structure around the center of the city—more than a mile in circumference, 20 to 25 feet in height, 14 to 30 feet thick. From the broad walkway on top, one sees the city at a sort of distance, and it is oddly beautiful. The hilltop business center is airy and sunlit, while other Irish cities tend to be dark and claustrophobic. The Bogside, a Catholic slum, begins beyond a clearing outside the wall to the west: row houses climb the opposite slope, a blue haze from every chimney pot drifts northward, the sun disappears beyond the whale-backed ridge above.

The Bogside, a Catholic enclave, opposes the city wall to the west.

The city wall was built to keep Catholics out, and that erstwhile function makes it an object of celebration and vilification even today. Its original purpose, one historian wrote, was "to assist the inhabitants in repelling any attack from the surrounding Celtic population, who were supposed to cherish anything but friendly feelings toward their neighbours." Living among the people they had dispossessed, the new settlers had reason to be fearful. Londonderry was not the only Protestant community to protect itself by walling out "the Irishry," nor did this happen only in the North. For a time in the seventeenth century, for instance, the town of Bandon, in County Cork, was also enclosed by a large wall. One of its gates is said to have borne the inscription "Turk, Jew, or Atheist may enter here; But not a Papist." A local wit replied: "Who wrote it, wrote it well; For the same is written on the Gates of Hell." That wall, however, was largely dismantled in 1688.

In that same year, Londonderry's city wall achieved a sort of immortality. An army loyal to the Catholic King James II of England was approaching the city, and the Protestant officer in charge of the garrison—whose name has been preserved in Protestant tradition as "the traitor Lundy"—showed little inclination to deny entry to the king's troops. The troops in question, however, were Catholics themselves, as well as being loyal to a Catholic king, and the Protestant citizenry feared that the notorious massacres of a Catholic uprising 47 years earlier would be repeated. Lundy was planning to give away the city, they said, "for a bab," a bun, nothing. At the last moment, thirteen apprentice boys, acting on their own, rushed down and closed the gates in the face of the approach-

*On a summer evening, children still sometimes play
beside the wall.*

ing army. The gates remained closed, under siege, for 105 days, until forces of the Protestant William of Orange, whom Parliament was to install as monarch in place of James II, came to the city's relief.

Today, the fraternal order known as the Apprentice Boys commemorates the closing of the gates each year by burning Lundy in effigy on the section of the city wall above the Bogside. It is an occasion for fireworks, drums, pipes, and, in the words of a Catholic writer, "the shrill ululation of fifes." Until recently, Lundy's effigy was always hanged from a column atop the wall honoring George Walker, a firebrand clergyman who suffered no Lundy-like ambivalence in his feelings toward Catholics. Walker's statue used to glower out at the Bogside from the top of the column, a Bible in one hand and a sword in the other. But it is recorded that on the night the Catholic Emancipation was signed in 1829, a strong wind arose and blew the sword out of his hand. The statue itself continued to stand, disarmed, until 1974. The same Catholic writer described it to me as "a symbol of thralldom, if you like, a constant reminder of the triumph of Protestantism over Catholicism." In the renewed troubles of the 1970s, the Irish Republican Army bombed the column unsuccessfully several times before it toppled in what a Bogsider described to me, with a smile, as a "strong wind."

Londonderry is of course known for strong winds of this sort, which may partly explain why the splendid promenade atop the city walls is desolate, even on a brilliant summer evening after prolonged rain. One meets a Swedish tourist there, or an Australian, but no Derrymen. The city center itself is abandoned by 6 P.M., with metal screens pulled down over every shopfront. Ubiquitous moni-

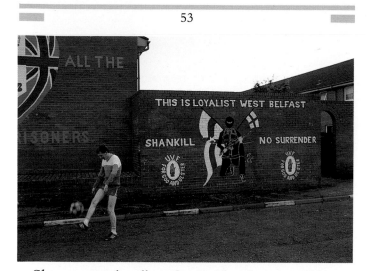

*Slogan-covered walls and painted curbstones proclaim
political and religious divisions in modern Belfast.*

tor cameras scrutinize every sidewalk. All is watchfulness, all movement correspondingly furtive. At the Apprentice Boys' Memorial Hall, just inside the city wall, older men with red skin and thickened middles slip up one at a time and knock lightly at a steel door with a peephole, as if seeking admission to a speakeasy. "There's always someone watching," one of them assures a visitor.

Every other building on Magazine Street has nonetheless been destroyed. The First Derry Presbyterian Church, bombed out and recently restored at a cost of £122,000, has been burned again, a victim of the cardinal law of real estate: location. There is nothing between Magazine Street and the Bogside but the wall, surmounted by an additional 30-foot height of chain-link fencing, and that is apparently not enough.

This is not to say the wall is no longer functional. In Londonderry, and in Belfast, too, walls are still used to keep Protestant and Catholic apart, and out of trouble. In Londonderry's ancient wall, the gates are movable steel panels of double thickness, painted a military green. In a demonstration, police can shift them to block off any of the gateways to the city center. In Belfast, in recent years, the so-called Peace Line has been built 20 feet high, out of corrugated metal and concrete block. It closes off through streets connecting the Falls Road and the Shankill Road so that these two working-class communities of opposed religions can pretend that they are not neighbors—a classic Irish response to inbred animosities.

Otherwise, though, the walls are mainly symbolic. They have become billboards for the often

LEFT
*Where symbolic proclamations don't keep apart troubled
areas of Belfast, corrugated metal fences do.*

OVERLEAF
*Hikers now use the top of the 22-mile-long Mourne
wall as a footpath through the mountains.*

cryptic slogans of the warring parties. On the pavement of the walltop in Londonderry, for example, someone has written: UFF RHC PAF LPA   IRA OUT. An outsider is likely to find the whole dispute deeply involuted, conducted in code, or by ritual. It has at times been customary, for example, for the Bogside community to mark the Anniversary of the Closing of the Gates by piling debris on its fires, in the hope that the outpouring of ashes will smother the finely dressed celebrants atop the wall. It is all liable to seem comically absurd, except that it is also routinely tragic.

At one point on the Londonderry city wall, several houses open directly onto the walltop promenade. They have been abandoned, evidently in a hurry. Coats still hang on hooks in the hall. A boarded-over window is marked with religious epithets. To the left, a seventeenth-century sentry post with arrow slits and a corbeled roof looks out at nothing. To the right, above Bishop's Gate, a modern sentry post of concrete blocks, enclosed in chain-link fencing and loops of barbed wire, also looks out at nothing, an empty street. The post is unmanned; a monitor camera there relays the scene to soldiers at a less vulnerable location. Not far from the two sentry posts, on a parapet, a graffito inquires: "Who the fuck are we?" Looking at the two sentry posts, the slogans, and the abandoned houses, a visitor is likely to feel that the people here have developed far too finely tuned a sense of who they are separately, and no sense at all of what they might have become together—a remarkable waste of 300 years.

Rolling fields, picked clean of their granite, define the landscape of County Down.

THE LOVELIEST PART OF THE NORTH, AND ONE OF THE less troubled, is the area known as The Mourne, an hour south of Belfast. Here every farmer builds walls, and a farmer's wife can tell a visitor not just the qualities of the different granites in the area, but their weight per cubic foot. "We're building more walls than ever," she says, "and better, too."

If the people of The Mourne build their walls bigger than ever now, one important reason is the steam shovel—beloved of modern Irish farmers, who know it by the brand name, JCB. In The Mourne, the JCBs paw across unreclaimed land and on up the mountain slopes, harvesting great piles of granite boulders. Some of these boulders are dumped into deep drainage trenches that run the length of the new fields to make the wet ground arable. Others are left in long piles, waiting for the builder to come and form them into walls. More often than not, the builder is Phelim Doran. As one farmer put it, "Phelim can build walls, there's no getting out of it." A considerable compliment in The Mourne.

"As I see it, it's blood pressure and oil pressure mixed," Doran says of his craft. The JCB noses a stone out of the pile, swings it over to the wall, and sets it roughly where it will go. Then Doran and the farmer he is working with nudge and sweat and worry it into place with crowbars and a hammer, until the stone gets a "bite" on its neighbors. Smaller wedges of stone, called "spallies," secure it in place.

In the terminology of County Down, what you see on the left is a ditch and what you see on the right is a wall.

This is perilous work, with boulders tottering at shoulder height, but it is also delicate. Doran likes his walls straight, and also tapered for durability. The bottom row of butt-stones, or "butters," may be a yard thick and up to 2 yards long, but the wall must narrow at the top to little more than a foot in thickness. The top must be level, and, especially with a wall built of smaller stones, the sides should be perfectly smooth. Ideally, the neighbors will notice and discuss it among themselves. "That wall has a skin on it," they will say.

But the work is also delicate in other ways. The walls, enclosing long, rectangular, sloping fields, are a natural extension of this rocky environment. Some of the walls are built directly over drainage ditches so that the stones seem to babble like streams. All of them are built to the dimensions of the livestock. Even a wall of great clumsy lumps of rock is likely to have a small, windowlike opening at ground level, so that sheep, but not cattle, can pass freely from one field to another. The walls are also built high enough so that when a cow wants to scratch her neck on a wall, she cannot nudge the top stones out of place. And they are built for shelter, to provide what Phelim Doran calls "easier living" for the animals. The gappy dry stone ditches are better at this, oddly, than a solid wall. The wind "plops over" the mortared wall, Doran says, but it filters through the dry ditch. A visitor who shelters against one of these walls on a windy afternoon may not perceive this; the wind seems to emerge from every gap with its bite intact. But a yard or so out, the needling rivulets of wind subside, and

BELOW

With sledges, crowbars, and the help of the almighty
JCB—a hydraulic shovel—wall-builder Phelim Doran
and Mourne farmer Dermot Trainor (in cap) wrestle
boulders into place.

RIGHT

The resulting ditch is herculean.

A father and child bring in their cow for its morning milking.

the air pauses instead of rushing breathlessly past. In this still pocket, the grass grows richer from the long sheltering of the animals. Surely in all this there is "wooing of earth," even if the farmer's chosen instrument of seduction is the JCB.

In Belfast, a student of agricultural history had conjectured that an outsider might not understand the Irish farmer's love of the land, his attachment to it, his territoriality—the way, for instance, he will know precisely how much of the thickness of a wall sits on his own land and how much on a neighbor's. It is not merely a matter of possessing the land, but of being possessed by it. The strength of this mutual bond is no weaker for Catholic or Protestant—the one having worked the land for generations with no right or title to it, the other still burdened with a settler's frame of mind: "No Surrender!" These farmers do not need to search for their roots; they are inescapable, sunk deep in the land of their forebears. And that rootedness shows up in their careful husbandry of the earth; the land has a kind of immortality for them.

This does not exempt the farmers from Northern Ireland's familiar political and religious differences, which they suffer and perhaps perpetuate like other Ulstermen. Doran recalls a riot some years ago, when Orangemen paraded noisily through a Catholic neighborhood. People tore stones from the walls and pelted them at one another. "It was neighbor against neighbor." But the next day Protestant and Catholic were back working together, brought to their senses by the necessities of tending to the land, and perhaps also by a pervasive sense of permanence about their way of life. That

On his farm of "five acres and a half," a farmer ties fresh-cut sheaves of oats.

sense informs every aspect of their lives. I asked one young farmer about a distinctive stone set into a new wall. He'd put it there, he said, "because it will look good in a hundred years." Later, going back to work, he added, "This ditch'll last five hundred or six hundred years. Maybe a thousand years. We'll be around again."

Nearby, an elderly farmer was bicycling out to one of his fields with a scythe over his shoulder. He parked his bike against a wall and went in among his oats through a metal gate. A dead crow hung there by its neck, a warning to living crows. The farmer had "five acres and a half," he said, as he sharpened his blade with a stone the shape of a corncob. He started to work at the mowing, his body dipping into the stroke, his arms turning across his torso with the curved handle of the scythe, the blade slicing cleanly through the oats. Then two steps forward and the same stroke repeated: *Thump, thump. Sweep. Thump, thump. Sweep.* At the end of the row, he turned and began bundling the cuttings into yellow sheaves, which he leaned against a wall to dry. In the distance, a cannon boomed to scare crows off someone else's fields. I asked him about his walls—an odd question, except to a Mourne farmer. He paused to survey them with satisfaction.

"Ah," he said. "They're everlasting."

CASHELS
CASTLES
AND DEMESNES

E NSCONCED
within an entry chamber in the thick stone
wall of a 1,000-year-old ring-fort on an abandoned island at the western edge of Europe,
a visitor is apt to contemplate the bloodiness
of Irish history. One squats where a guard
once waited, in a stone niche above a crawlway entrance. The chamber is high enough

PRECEDING PAGES

*The fifteenth-century ruins of Kilbarron Castle stand on
a cliff above the sea near Ballyshannon, County
Donegal (pages 64, 65); no one lives on Inishmurray
anymore, but the cursing stones remain intact. Belief in
their supernatural powers is undiminished.*

RIGHT

*A tumbledown wall at a graveyard where the people
of Inishmurray buried their dead during more than
a millennium.*

for the guard to raise a spear or a stone and dash it down into the brains of an unwelcome intruder, leaving the corpse to block the entry. Overhead, a "murdering hole" in the roof of the chamber affords the same opportunity to defenders on top of the wall, should the guard somehow fail. From the crawlway entrance, it is an uphill scramble to the interior of the fort. An intruder who somehow got that far would emerge helpless at the feet of those inside: the scholars and saints of a highly regarded Christian monastery.

It may appear that the medieval monks of Inishmurray, an island with no real harbor, 4½ miles off the coast of County Sligo, overestimated their need for defense. Indeed, it might easily seem that all Ireland suffered for much of its history from an exaggerated urge to close itself off from the world. Stout and ancient walls everywhere form such points of refuge, of eremitic retreat, and of defense. Not only are there 30,000 raths, but there are also numerous hill and promontory forts (built mostly in the first millennium A.D., some of them in easy sight of one another); medieval monasteries established in former military strongholds; round towers with their doorways 15 feet above ground; thirteenth-century Norman castles so plentiful that there is hardly a spot in Ireland where one is not visible; and walled towns (forty of them by Elizabethan times). Even eighteenth-century Georgian homes built by landlords for splendid leisure are guarded by metal shutters and by stone walls as much as 10 miles long. This unruly instinct for walls shows itself at times even now. A government

Within the cashel on Inishmurray, St. Molaise's chapel
stands with its original stone roof intact, sheltering the
blood stains of noblemen slaughtered there in 802.

official recently threw up a high wall around his retreat on the Shannon River. The effect, alas, was not aesthetic. He used concrete block, of which a wall–builder I met remarked concisely: "It gives you nothing, like, only dimension." All of these were built to provide security, or at least a sense of it.

The walls are there because of the wildness of Irish history. On Inishmurray, despite a wall that is 8 feet thick and up to 14 feet high, Norse raiders slaughtered the monks in 802. Within the oval cashel (an Irish term for a stone ring-fort), the monks had built beehive huts and a small chapel, which survive. Subsequent residents of the island, into the twentieth century, maintained that "blood spots" on the stones of the chapel were from eighty sons of noblemen slain in the Norse raid. Certain specks, they believed, were the blood of the last reigning abbot. Skeptics said these specks were merely lichen and could be scraped away with a knife. The islanders agreed, but said the specks always came back in the same pattern.

The Norse raiders were a continual source of terror to the Irish over two centuries—and, afterward, in memory. Not long after the destruction of Inishmurray, an Irish poet wrote:

> There's a wicked wind tonight,
> Wild upheaval in the sea;
> No fear now that the Viking hordes
> Will terrify me.

*A restored beehive hut and the abandoned houses of
Inishmurray look across to Ben Bulben in County Sligo.*

But before and after the Vikings, the Irish wreaked holy terror among themselves. Society organized itself along feudal lines, into communities called *tuatha,* some of them quite small but each ruled by a so-called king. The *tuatha* banded together into loose "overkingdoms," dominated by the king of the largest *tuath.* The number of these overkingdoms ranged from five to eight. No kingship was ever directly hereditary, and no king or dynasty was ever able to assert control over all Ireland, though many tried. Instead of coalescing into nationhood, the Irish thus endured permanent rivalries among their leading families, making for disorder at best and sometimes for bloody warfare.

The Irish to this day have an unnatural ability to sustain a quarrel, though their disputes now tend to be characterized less by physical violence than by the giving of small, devastating slights and by a corresponding readiness to imagine that slights have been given. The involuted quality of this give-and-take is perhaps a product of the long Irish memory and the strong attachment to place. For example, in a Donegal village where certain families converted to Protestantism during the Famine in exchange for soup, their descendants are still known as "Soupers." In a community in County Cork, similarly, the people designated a branch of the Sheehan family who were "Soupers" by mispronouncing their name as "Shay-han." In 1985, more than 135 years after the Famine, a young priest told me that he came near to having his nose broken when he unwittingly applied the wrong pronunciation to a fellow seminarian. A truly extreme example of this phenomenon was reported to me by James Delaney, a folklorist. Some years ago, he was visiting an elderly storyteller in County

Ten miles of rolling sea separate the Skellig Rocks from mainland County Kerry.

Offaly. "I told him my name was Delaney, and he said, 'Ah, it was you and your crowd that attacked Brian Boru's army on the way back from the Battle of Clontarf.' " (Brian Boru, the greatest of the Irish kings, was killed after defeating the Norse at Clontarf in 1014. Anno Domini, of course.)

It may be that the Irish landscape did not foster feelings of security or of national unity. The rich central lowlands were originally swamp and forest, home to wolves and other predators (about an eighth of Ireland was forest as late as 1600). The upland countryside, meanwhile, seldom offered broad perspectives suitable for defensive lookouts. In some areas, notably in a long belt separating Ulster from the rest of Ireland, the low hills, called drumlins, were grouped as close together as eggs in a basket and formed a physical and cultural divide. Along the coast, the many inlets of the sea offered avenues for trade, but also for murderous surprise attacks. The cry of havoc could be as sudden as a gale blowing in off the Atlantic. Hence, perhaps, the walled fortifications of every variety.

But these defensive considerations aside, there was also something otherworldly about the Irish withdrawal behind walls. The circular form of many of the early enclosures is itself suggestive. In *Man and His Landscape in Ireland,* F. H. A. Aalen writes that this form "appears to have been the secular development of an extremely ancient religious tradition, and the forerunners of the raths are perhaps the sacred enclosures erected around megalithic burial sites. . . ." Such burial sites, with enclosures built of stone, are known as "court tombs," and 330 survive in Ireland, mostly in the North, where they were apparently built by early farmers. Stone circles, for burials or other ritual purposes, also

To further ensure their isolation from the world, the monks of Skellig Michael built their walled-in monastery on a precipice 650 feet above sea level.

abound; more than 90 are known in counties Cork and Kerry alone. Their function is lost, but presumably they were places where the local population gathered in conclave, to seek divine assistance and to utter pagan incantations.

The cashel at Inishmurray evokes an eerie sense of such rituals, despite its long Christian history. A dry stone altar, said to have been built 2,000 years ago by the adherents of a sun-worshipping religion, dominates the courtyard. The altar has been Christianized. Stones inscribed with crosses have been driven into its top. (Two of these crosses are also chrismatories, and each of them still has a stone cap, the nippled bottom of which fits snugly into a small font scooped out of the top of the cross.) But the altar retains a pagan name, the *Clocha Breacha,* which means "the cursing stones."

The round, speckled cursing stones are still there, on top of the altar, in front of the crosses. They have in fact been inscribed with crosses themselves. (Indeed, it is quite possible the stones were at times employed by the monks, cursing and Christianity being closely allied in Ireland. Giraldus Cambrensis, himself a clergyman, though hardly an unbiased observer, noted "that the saints of this country seem to be of a vindictive case of mind.") The ritual for invoking the stones to bring vengeance on an enemy is well known; it was employed as recently as World War II, by a visiting Englishwoman, against Hitler. Patrick Heraughty, who grew up on Inishmurray before the islanders gave up the hard life there and moved to the mainland in 1947, has described the maledictive rite in detail. It was an elaborate undertaking, made more serious by the knowledge that a person who

A gallery grave in the wilds of Connemara.

LEFT
*Gravestones, beehive huts, and walls enclosing
handmade gardens are the only remnants of the Skellig
Michael cloister.*

invoked the stones without proper cause would suffer his own curse. The supplicant spent nine days in preparation, the first three in absolute fast, the second three taking only one meal, and the last three eating normally—a reversal of customary religious practice. On the day itself, the supplicant walked the stations of the island counterclockwise, against the direction of the sun. At the *Clocha Breacha,* he made three circuits, turning over each of the round stones on the altar. All this, as Heraughty wrote, had "decidedly pagan connotations."

Cursing stones occur elsewhere in Ireland, and they figure, along with the circular enclosure, in an incident from an early Irish manuscript. Pagan priests, angered by a king's conversion to Christianity, are said to have turned the stones against him. In the nineteenth century, Sir Samuel Ferguson based part of a poem on the incident:

> They loosed their curse against the king,
> They cursed him in his flesh and bones,
> And daily in their mystic ring,
> They turned the maledictive stones.

Somewhat more recently, in 1884, the islanders of Inishmurray turned the cursing stones against a

Stout, fortresslike gate posts often defend even modest farms in County Antrim.

RIGHT

In Sligo, as in much of Ireland, a house is not properly finished until the property is "closed up" with a neat fence.

gunboat, the H.M.S. *Wasp,* sent with a detachment of soldiers and police to collect rents they deemed unfair. The gunboat was wrecked, and all but six of those on board drowned.

The outsider might at first read only superstition and political impotence into such episodes—the powerless within their antique forts shielding themselves behind pagan ritual and a few old stones. On the spot, though, I hesitated even to touch the stones, and I came away impressed with the Irish faith in the power of words and intentions in their proper setting. It is tempting to see in this the origin of the otherwise perverse tradition, among Irish political prisoners, of starving themselves to bring the force of their own deaths down upon the heads of their enemies.

NOTHING COULD SEEM FARTHER FROM THESE MYS-tic rings and their dark business than the great demesnes established in the eighteenth and nineteenth centuries. After the armies of Oliver Cromwell ravaged the countryside and after William of Orange triumphed at the Battle of the Boyne in 1690, English control of Ireland became secure. The cashels and castles were for the first time obsolete. The landlords came down from their Norman towers and shucked off the gloomy fortifications of the past. Over the next 150 years, they graced the Irish countryside with a spectacular assortment of Palladian, Neoclassical, and Greek Revival houses. Concern

Round, sea-washed stones form a diminutive wall in
Mullaghmore, County Sligo.

for strategic location gave way to a taste for tree-lined entries and grand panoramas. The architecture of defense was forgotten, except as a spur to fantasy in the Gothic Revival, when crenelations concealed chimney tops and arrow slits lit the dairy. (It is interesting, however, that the estate houses often sheltered farm buildings within their wings. In *Irish Houses and Castles,* Desmond Guinness and William Ryan theorize that this was a way to extend the façade and make it more impressive. But they add, "It may equally have been reassuring to have the animals close at hand, as in previous centuries they always had been. . . .")

The demesne walls that now encircled almost every estate were psychological rather than defensive barriers. They certainly had practical functions: keeping the deer in the deer park, for instance, and keeping the tenants' cattle out. Mainly, though, they served to keep the tenants themselves out, to screen the estate off from the view of "the gazing rustic," to create within their bounds a comfortable and well-ordered world apart. At Carton, in County Kildare, 1,000 acres were thus enclosed within a wall 5 miles long, and between 1738 and 1757, an elaborate park was developed according to notions, then current in England, of the naturalistic garden.

Landlords wasted comparatively little time on the walls themselves, except for the gate. This project they often undertook with special enthusiasm, as a display of power and prosperity (the house itself usually being well hidden from the road). Guinness and Ryan relate the story of a gentleman named Smyth in County Westmeath, whose enormous gates, surmounted by a stone unicorn, led to

*Fanciful trappings on a farm wall in Annalong,
County Down.*

a "rather plain" house. He was properly nicknamed "Smyth With the Gates." This annoyed his son, who eventually moved the gates elsewhere and was thereafter known as "Smyth Without the Gates." Apart from the gates, though, the demesne walls were distinguished mainly by their sprawling size.

In one remarkable wall, however, a landlord left a monument to his own flawed character. The so-called Jealous Wall, a sham ruin 100 feet or more long and perhaps half as high, stands on the grounds of Belvedere House near Mullingar. Robert Rochfort, Baron Belfield, built it in about 1750. The story connected with it begins in 1736, when Belfield, then twenty-eight, married Mary Molesworth, the talented and beautiful sixteen-year-old daughter of a Dublin viscount. He greeted the birth of their first child, a girl, with disappointment; of their second, a son whom he named after the king, with lavish celebration; and of two subsequent sons, with indifference. By all accounts, Belfield was a mean and unappreciative husband. He spent much of his time attending to his own pleasures in Dublin or London, while his wife languished in the relative isolation of County West-meath. On his forays into the world, he left behind a local woman who may have been his mistress and spy, a second woman, on the household staff, with whose affections he had apparently dallied, and two brothers living in the neighborhood.

One of the brothers, George Rochfort, was a malignant specimen, born to play the part of Iago. The other brother, Arthur, and his wife were considerably more sympathetic, and they became Mary's companions. In time, the spies reported, Arthur also became Mary's lover. Belfield denounced

RIGHT

On the walls of a great estate in County Westmeath,
the fanciful trappings are sometimes live.

OVERLEAF

The owner of Belvedere House built the sham ruin
known as "the Jealous Wall" to block the view of his
brother's estate.

her, and George, who had disliked her from the start, produced alleged "love letters" that had somehow come into his possession. The gossip in London, reported by the Earl of Egmont in his diary entry for May 2, 1743, was that Mary not only admitted the transgression with Arthur, but said "that her last child was by him, and that she had no pleasure with any man like that she had with him." This statement, and the love letters, may have been a convenient fabrication by her enemies; Mary herself maintained on her deathbed that she was innocent. Alternatively, says Leo Daly, a local historian, she may have been advised by friends that an admission would help to win her a divorce.

Instead, though, Belfield locked her up in a garret of their house in Gaulstown. None of her friends came to her assistance, a circumstance Daly attributes to the "absolute power" Belfield exercised in the district and to "the reluctance of the age to interfere between man and wife." When Mary escaped twelve years later to Dublin, her own father rebuked her for incest and for being no better than an undeserving bastard child. He returned her to Gaulstown, where she remained imprisoned for another eighteen years.

Belfield meanwhile went to live at Belvedere House, a "fishing lodge" of lavish proportions that he had built for himself on the shores of Lough Ennel, 6 miles from Gaulstown. The Jealous Wall rose there, according to local tradition, to screen off the view to his brother's house less than a half-mile away. It is easy to imagine how this view, with its bitter associations, might have troubled him. Off to one side, as he stood at his front door or in his bedroom, it would have tugged his glance away

The Irish bury their dead not just within graveyard walls, but within the walls of ruined churches and abbeys, like this one from County Leitrim.

from the excellent vista of Lough Ennel, constantly freshening the memory of his wife's betrayal or, perhaps, of his own unworthy suspicions. But lest one lapse improbably into sympathy, history serves as a corrective: the neighboring house belonged not to Arthur, but to George. In time, it seems, Belfield had a falling out with his fellow conspirator; the vindictiveness of the two brothers turned in on each other. According to one theory, the source of Belfield's jealousy was not Arthur's betrayal, but George's house, which was larger and more grand than his own. Arthur meanwhile was ruined and appears to have died in prison. On Belfield's death, Mary emerged from her confinement looking haggard and unearthly, her voice seldom rising above a broken whisper.

If it were the only incident of its kind, this story would be merely horrifying. But the unlikely combination of stone walls and marital infidelity turns up again in County Westmeath, and it suggests that the landlords too were susceptible to the defensive psychology of the countryside, the urge to isolate oneself, and the propensity to seek vindictive refuge within the "mystic ring." In Tristernagh in 1807, "a gambler, duellist, and spendthrift," Sir John Piers by name, wagered that he could seduce Lady Cloncurry, the wife of a friend and benefactor. He won the bet. But Lord Cloncurry sued and obtained a judgment of £20,000 against him. Assailed by creditors and by the prying eyes of neighbors (including one Richard Malone, who fashioned himself "Lord Sunderlin of Baronstown"), Piers did a remarkable thing: he built a cottage enclosed by a high wall "to protect himself from the minions of justice."

The ancient ring fort of Staigue in County Kerry.

"Now I can only build my walls and die," Piers says, in a poem by the recent British Laureate, John Betjeman. He builds "against the vista and the duns [his creditors], a mighty wall against the rain":

> And from the North, lest you, Malone, should spy me,
> You, Sunderlin of Baronstown, the peer,
> I'll fill your eye with all the stone that's by me
> And live four-square protected in my fear.

His strategy did not work. His land was sold off by the Encumbered Estates Court, and he died penniless. What he lacked, perhaps, was a cursing stone and the knowledge of its use. His walled refuge, like the cashel at Inishmurray, is today only a quaint ruin.

Ruin was, indeed, also the fate of many of the great houses. Some landlords abandoned their estates as land reform at the end of the nineteenth century made them unprofitable. Some houses were destroyed in rebellion and civil war between 1916 and 1922. Others survived, only to have their roofs stripped off by their owners, who mistakenly believed that ruin was the only way to avoid heavy property taxes. In many places, the demesne walls and the gate cottages are all that survive. They are a peculiar, ironic memorial to an age.

The walls had been built, in the words of folklorist Kevin Danaher, "to keep the common herd in their proper place and ensure milord's privacy." They were built around vast acreages obtained by evicting whoever lived there; they cushioned the gentry from contact with a resentful, dispossessed people, different in race, religion, and language. If the more benevolent landlords were saddened by the necessity of "shutting Ireland out," still they must have been relieved and comforted by the fact of being walled in, especially as the system that supported them drove the peasantry deeper into poverty and squalor. It is striking that when the Famine came, bringing horror to every doorstep, those landlords who helped their tenants often chose, as a form of relief work, to make their demesne walls higher.

"Now," Danaher has written, "the farmer's cows graze on milord's pleasure gardens and shelter in the ruins of the Great House" — an irony of which every Irish farmer is assuredly, contentedly, aware.

One day in eastern County Galway, I came across a folk tale on this point. I had been assured, by Danaher himself, that the walls did not figure in Irish folklore. An affable man, scrupulous without being pedantic, he had broken the bad news to me graciously, but firmly: in a lifetime of research around Ireland, he hadn't heard a single folk tale about stone walls. On the other hand, he added professorially, there also weren't any stories about the potato. Some things attracted folklore — tobacco, for instance, with its supposed medicinal effects. Other things, like the walls, were too much a part of everyday life, as commonplace as the sky and the grass. This was daunting news. What I looked forward to among the Irish was their way of making a point, about walls or whatever, by telling a story — or rather, their way of telling a story, and the devil take the point.

OVERLEAF
A roadside shrine in a walled enclosure in Innishannon,
County Cork.

But Danaher seemed to be right; there were no folk tales about walls. I asked everywhere. Finally, though, someone sent me to Willie Leahy, a horseman from Loughrea. "He's a great one for talk," someone had promised. "He'd talk the water up a duck's arse. You want a week if you go talking to him." In fact, it took much of a day, as he chewed over the notion of walls and picked at his memory. Then, sprawled on a stoop with his three-year-old daughter at his knee, he told a story. The Irish were accustomed to the landlords using the demesne walls to exclude them from their former land. Here, instead, was a tale in which the people used the walls to take land away from a landlord.

"There was this woman had no place to sow potatoes," he began. "No place at all, at all. And she had a family. And she went to the big estate and she said, 'Will you ever give me a plot of land to sow potatoes?'

"And they said, 'No, no, we have no time for that.' And she kept begging—'The family is starving'—and they said, 'No, no.'

"So she said, 'Won't you even give me the ground I can build a wall around in a night?' And they said, 'Yes,' just to be rid of her. So she communicated this to friends and neighbors and they all turned out with horses and carts and gathered stones from all over the area. And whether it was 300 or 400 acres that the wall enclosed, I can't say, and what the Man Above was doing.

"Now," Leahy concluded, slapping his knee, "are there any more lies I can tell you?"

T H E
WEST

W ALLS?" THE

drinker asked, after I'd explained my business that Sunday noon in the pub at St. Brigid's Well. "*Stone* walls?" he said. I nodded, and a conversational counterattack took shape in his mind.

If I wanted to talk about walls, he began, had I heard what a general in the invading army of Oliver Cromwell once said about the landscape hereabouts? He drew himself up in the swaybacked posture of oral tradition and cast about in the sodden corners of his memory. "The place is so barren," he began, "that there isn't water enough to drown a man, or wood enough to hang a man . . ."—here memory momentarily faltered—". . . or earth enough to bury a man." He paused for dramatic effect, then added the traditional postscript: "*But there are stones enough to kill any man.*"

This is, after all, not a bad description of the whole Irish landscape. But it is especially apt around Galway Bay, from Liscannor, in County Clare, around to Clifden, at the tip of the Connemara Peninsula. It is a world of limestone on the south side of the bay and of granite on the north. The Aran Islands, across the mouth of the bay, bridge the two areas and, stone-mad, borrow from both— a landscape of gray limestone outcrops heaped with limestone boulders and a smattering of granite erratics dumped there by receding glaciers. To the north of Connemara, counties Mayo and Sligo are only somewhat less littered with rock. There is really only one thing a farmer could do with all this stone: kill himself building walls, to clear the land.

"Stones," says old Cabot, in Eugene O'Neill's *Desire Under the Elms*. "I picked 'em up an' piled 'em into walls. Ye kin read the years of my life in them walls, every day a hefted stone, climbin' over the hills up and down, fencin' in the fields that was mine." Cabot was talking about his "fields o' stones" in New England, but the words apply as well in the West of Ireland. Over the centuries, farmers fencing in their fields have divided and subdivided this countryside into a vast jigsaw puzzle several thousand square miles in area. In a terrain where one geologist writes of "grass appearing only as

A farm below the Maamturk Mountains in County Galway.

veins amongst the rocks," every arable snippet of land has at one time or another been walled in and exploited. On the bleak purple mountainsides, the walls climb up even into the clouds, and come down again on the other side.

More remarkable than the walls themselves is the number of people these tiny fields supported — and the manner in which they lived. For all the hard feelings, the giving and taking of slights, the animosities kept alive through generations, Irish farmers worked within a remarkably cooperative and egalitarian society.

The basis of that society was the so-called rundale system, a relic of pre-enclosure days that came to be more or less permanently embodied in the walled fields of the eighteenth and nineteenth centuries. In rundale, farmers living in a given area worked the land collectively. Instead of holding contiguous fields in a compact family farm, each family held scattered patches of land all around the cultivated area, "mixed throughother" with the fields of neighboring families. Originally, this was done to give each family its equal share of every quality of land, from rich tillage to the sparsest pasturage of the outfield. In places, to further ensure fair division of the land, fields changed hands at regular intervals, a system that has been called "changedale" or "morrowingdale."

Communal farming of this sort appears to have coexisted with scattered individual farms from an early time. Individual farms may, in fact, have grown into communal farms as families expanded,

Along the coast, walls sometimes enclose more than their original builders intended.

only to splinter off into individual farms again when the cluster of families reached an unwieldy size. These clusters of houses, called "clachans," are still visible in a few places, the cottages bunched together in the words of one early visitor, "like a child's box of bricks spilled on the floor." In the eighteenth and nineteenth centuries, they were common, especially west of a line from Londonderry to Cork. As the Irish were pushed steadily westward, rundale became the model, conscious or otherwise, for dividing up the new land. Where the boundary lines in open-field days had been raised strips of sod, or mearing stones set at intervals, the landscape in places like Connemara necessitated that they be stone walls—not just to get the stones off the ground or to provide shelter, but to help farmers keep track of their holdings. This became increasingly difficult as the population built up and, in effect, grew in on itself.

Between 1791 and 1841, when the escape valve of emigration was almost nonexistent, the population of Ireland rose from less than 5 million people to more than 8. Much of this increase took place among the poor, and the highest densities were often concentrated on the poorest land, a fact that manifested itself in the walls and the fields: until the Famine, it was customary for a father's land to be subdivided equally among his male heirs—a characteristically fair system (within its decidedly non-feminist context), but one that was ultimately self-destructive.

In one typical case, from County Donegal, a compact 205-acre plot evolved, between the late

The land hunger of the nineteenth century forced
farmers to clear and cultivate the most remote and
worthless bits of land.

eighteenth and mid-nineteenth centuries, from a single-family farm into a clachan of 29 families with holdings fragmented into 422 separate plots. In County Mayo in this century, the Congested Districts Board broke up a clachan of 56 families whose land, Estyn Evans reported, "was scattered in 1,500 fragments, some of them no more than a dozen square yards in area. A two-acre holding was split into eighteen tiny plots, and on the average twenty-seven lots were held by each farm. . . ." The story is told of two brothers on a farm that was already too small for further subdivision. One of them was to stay home and eke a living from the land, while the other of necessity was to seek his fortune elsewhere. But on the eve of the departure, the one broke down and begged the other to stay and share the land. They went out the next day and divided it up with a measuring tape. In the province of Connaught (encompassing counties Galway, Mayo, Sligo, Leitrim, and Roscommon), 90 percent of the farm holdings in 1841 were smaller than 15 acres. Farms of 1 to 5 acres vastly outnumbered all others.

The sole reason so many people could live on so little land—and the key factor, along with rundale, in shaping the jigsaw puzzle of the Irish West—was the potato. The Irish method of cultivation, in raised beds or ridges dug with a shovel, was suitable to small fields only and, as such, was extremely productive. One acre of land planted in potatoes could feed a family of six, and their livestock, for a year. This statistic is considerably more impressive than it may at first sound: potatoes were practically the only thing most Irish families ate. Arthur Young, an eighteenth-century traveler in Ireland,

Donkeys are terrible rogues; walls don't always keep
them in their place.

reported that the Irish diet consisted of potatoes and milk for ten months of the year and potatoes and salt for two. Per capita consumption averaged 8 pounds a day, and probably up to 12 for an adult male. In the nineteenth century, the latter figure rose to 14 pounds.

This is not a diet most people would freely choose. The Irish did so for a variety of practical reasons, apart from nutritional value and ease of cultivation. The potato, introduced in about 1600, had the great virtue, during the Elizabethan and Cromwellian wars, of being hidden in the ground where armies were less likely to see and destroy it. In times of peace, under the landlord system, it had the additional advantage of being far easier to store than other crops. Tenants had no right to compensation for the building of barns—needed to store cereals—or for other improvements to the land. Such improvements in fact often triggered demands for increased rent. A farmer who grew potatoes, which could be stored in the ground, incurred no such risk. "In the potato," one historian wrote, "the people discovered a new weapon with which to withstand the oppression of their conquerors." But it also became the means of their degradation. The Irish were desperate to keep a hold on the land. By subsisting at the minimal level of the potato, they could meet higher rents and work for lower pay than would, for example, a Scottish or English settler. The potato kept body, soul, and family together on the land as the Irish slid down into squalor.

Much of the marginal land enclosed and cultivated in the difficult years before the Famine is now abandoned again. (Some of it was cleared in wholesale evictions by landlords intent on replacing rundale

PRECEDING PAGES
At the Cliffs of Moher, a wall "a mile long, a yard high, and an inch thick."

with a more rational system of land organization in the 1850s.) Farmers today shelter their livestock in the ruins of not just the old estate houses but also the most humble and remote cabins, their roofs now rotted away and their hearths long since cold. The field walls survive around them, thousands and thousands of stones piled into useless ribbons running across gray hills no one would care to cultivate today. In many places, the land is still furrowed from pre-Famine potato ridges, as if someone a hundred years ago raked a huge comb across the slopes, for reasons we can scarcely imagine.

THE FIELD WALLS OF THE WEST OF IRELAND COME IN several distinctive types, and the pub at St. Brigid's Well is as good a place as any to learn about one of the more remarkable of them. Next door stands a great memorial column to a nineteenth-century landlord, a man of obvious Irish background named Cornelius O'Brien. It commemorates his "warm-hearted liberality," his efforts in promoting "the happiness and comfort of his people," and his "forethought in providing for the accommodation of strangers visiting the magnificent scenery of this neighborhood." A 1961 guidebook notes of this monument only that O'Brien "compelled his tenants to pay for it." Of his "warm-hearted liberality," the locals remember that he denied a priest coming to say Mass the use of a shortcut across his lands. (For this the priest of course cursed

O'Brien's estate, saying the trees would wither and crows fly through his house. And, of course, the curse came true, as anyone can see from St. Brigid's Well.) Finally, of O'Brien's "accommodation of strangers," a story is told that he once bet a visitor that he could show him a dry stone wall "a mile long, a yard high, and an inch thick."

"He lost, of course?" I said, to the drinkers in the pub.

Another man, obviously not born in the neighborhood, leaned over to say, sotto voce, "These boys don't lose their bets."

In fact, O'Brien's wall, or one like it, stood not ten minutes away, up on the Cliffs of Moher. Maybe it wasn't a mile long, but it was an inch thick and a yard or more high, made up entirely of flagstones set upright, their ends overlapping like a line of playing cards. The flags, used in field walls all around the area, are "mudstone," formed when the land (now 600 feet above the Atlantic at the cliffs) was the bottom of a warm, shallow sea; on the surface of the upright flags, wormy tracings preserved in fossil form make a sort of Celtic weave.

These flags occur only in the Liscannor area, but the two other wall types found there occur throughout Ireland. Double walls are the sturdiest type and the easiest to build, with two parallel stacks of stone tending to support each other and a loose filling of spall in between. But the single wall is more spectacular, a delicate fretwork of stone running across the fields, with gaps through which the passerby can see greens and golds and the sunlight dancing on the sea.

Farm children near Ballyvaughan, County Clare.

The distinction between wall types became pertinent later that afternoon, when I stopped my car and went for a walk in the rocky section of County Clare known as the Burren. Here the earth is all limestone, formed by sedimentation under the sea and forced up to the surface, then ground flat as a bed by glaciers, and finally littered with rocky debris as the ice retreated. Gray stone walls ran across fields of gray pavement. Three bullocks stood in an enclosure, looking as if they could not find cud to chew. But beyond them was a grassy strip between a wall and the sea, and it beckoned the casual visitor. I had hardly begun to stroll there, though, when I saw—in Ireland! on Sunday!—a naked man and a naked woman sprawling in the grass, and the two of them clearly feeling the full heat of the day. Two thoughts occurred, as I spun around and hurried away. The first was a fragment of seventeenth-century Irish verse about the war between the sexes:

> . . . the devil take her and all she showed!
> I found her myself on the public road,
> On the naked earth with a bare backside
> And a Garus turf-cutter astride!

The second, suggesting a considerable evolution in the Irish position on sex, was a bumper sticker I'd seen on the road that morning: "Sally Does It with a Harp."

A field gate in County Mayo.

When I finally looked back, having circled up toward the car, I saw that between me and the happy couple there was a wall—a single wall, to be precise—whose gaps revealed the rhythmic waving of the woman's delicately upraised feet, on which she still wore white ankle socks.

THERE HAS ALWAYS BEEN A RICH ABUNDANCE OF LIFE within the fields. The walls form the winding, higgledy-piggledy framework within which the highly localized doings of the small farming communities run their course. To an outsider, they at first look impassable, perhaps even a little hostile. More often than not, they lack anything like a gate or entry. A visitor naturally wonders how that 1,200-pound cow got inside. But the lack of gates is merely practical. Any opening would let in the sea wind, lift up the soil, disturb the crops, discomfort the "beasts." Gates also require wood, which is rare in the West. A few farmers will turn an old car door into a makeshift gate. But the traditional way to bring livestock into or out of a field is by way of the gap, a small section where stones are stacked loosely, to be taken down and then thrown up again after the animals have passed through. Farmers accustomed all their lives to stone seem to open and close gaps not just quickly, but without effort.

Getting humans in and out might seem more unwieldy. The gap is of course too much bother. But

With the help of a stile, a farmer crosses a 10-foot-thick
wall near Athlone.

single walls look too fragile to climb. It's not just that you can see right through them, but the stones on top are often left loose to topple when sheep attempt to jump them. (The fright this gives them is said to work better than barbed wire.) Sometimes, despite numerous testimonials to their strength, a whole wall will topple underfoot. "I had the experience of having a wall fall on me," a rather befuddled hitchhiker told me one day. "I went over and it followed me and caught me on the big toes. I had to go to a chiropodist. It wasn't a great success. My nails grew t'ick afterwards. At least the ones that was tampered with."

The falling wall is a peril not lightly to be risked, but in fact there is an art to crossing even a fragile single wall: you mount the wall as if it were a horse. Galway men are said to be especially adept at this, finding a stone low down on the near side and another on the far side, so they don't ever touch any of the loose stones at the top. A Galway man crossing a wall thus looks momentarily like a cowboy standing in the stirrups.

Getting back and forth easily is of course important if you have to go milk the cow every evening, or tend to the crops. In the past, neighbors regularly visited back and forth across the walls, sending a son over to help a neighbor make hay or having the neighbor in to help with the thatching of a roof. James Delaney, who has spent his life gathering folklore in and around County Roscommon, explained some of this way of life to me one afternoon. From his home we drove to an abandoned church in the middle of a large, well-cropped field. During the time of the Penal Laws against Catho-

Folklorist James Delaney of County Roscommon.

lics, he said, the English tolerated the building of churches only well off the roads, out of sight. Alternative routes and shortcuts through fields and over walls became known as Mass paths, though they might also lead to a graveyard, a shop, a local pub, a well. "An old man in south Offaly told me that in his young days — that'd be before the bicycle — there were stiles in every field and the people very seldom used the high roads. They always cut through the fields."

Delaney then taught me another secret of crossing walls: the stiles are still there, though they no longer get quite as much use. They are mostly flat stones projecting out of the sides of a wall, arranged to form an easy, if almost invisible, staircase up and over. There is something surreal about the sight of a farmer ascending a wall in this way. "Climbing a ditch" is just the right phrase for it. But perhaps it was even more so in the past, when the Mass paths didn't always lead to church.

"There was a time," said Delaney, "when the law was you had to travel 3 miles from your bed in order to get a drink on Sunday, and the police would measure the distance. This was done as late as 1942 in Wexford." The logic, or illogic, of it was that only travelers should need to refresh themselves with strong drink on the Lord's Day. "Well," Delaney continued, "a man might have a pub that was only a mile and a half from him across the fields, but he was okay because it was three miles by the road. Or the path might lead to a shebeen, a place where liquor was sold without license."

Indeed, the path might lead to a wall itself, in which liquor and the illegal still for making it were often hidden. "*Poteen,*" Kevin Danaher had remarked when I visited him in Dublin. "Jars of it. I'll

Old cartwheel rims were sometimes straightened to make gates like this one in County Clare.

LEFT

Bottleneck at a sheep creep in County Galway.

tell you a case in north Mayo." He held an open hand in front of his face as if about to sneeze, eyes squeezed shut as he recollected the details. "A fellow who was slightly inebriated had hidden a jar of the stuff, or two gallons, in a wall, and couldn't remember where it was, and he pulled down several walls trying to find it. I was there the day it was found, twenty-two years later. It had matured beautifully, I understand." Under the influence of such stuff, even Galway wall climbers must have thanked God for stiles. Also, perhaps, for sheep creeps, a less vertiginous way of crossing walls.

A sheep creep is a windowlike opening in the wall at ground level with a lintel across the top. In the West, the farmers used the creeps to wean lambs, by encouraging them to wander away from their mothers into nearby fields. In Clare, though, a farmer showed me a creep too low for even a lamb. It was for rabbits, he said, and setting a net there used to be a reliable way of catching your dinner. In Roscommon, another farmer showed me a sheep creep 10 feet long, through a wall that was like an elongated bunker, a great dump for stones gathered by hand out of the fields. (Such massive walls are probably the result of periodic bursts of land clearing over hundreds of years. Like the rings of a tree, each new skin would tell an archeologist something about the life and the economic standing of its builders.) Despite the utterly unmilitary setting, this particular wall was well crafted enough to do credit to a castle. Or a pyramid. Smooth stepping-stones formed stiles, and the sheep creep running through the wall was like the tunnel entrance to a passage tomb.

But the sheep creeps are mostly blocked up with stone now. The farmers for one reason or another

*In Castlemaine, County Kerry, father and son—
both named Timmy O'Connor—manage their sheep
farm together.*

RIGHT

*The walls do not figure much in Irish lore. Asked for an
instance, Oughterard schoolgirl Eileen Walsh pondered
and replied: "Humpty Dumpty?"*

find it easier not to use them much anymore. The farmers' children often find it easier not to farm at all. They have become accountants and salespeople, and they whiz across the landscape in Toyota Corollas, tuned in to disc jockeys with American accents. The stiles and the sheep creeps are forgotten, and the Mass paths are all gone to nettles.

THE WAY OF LIFE THAT IS SOMETIMES DISMISSED IN Dublin as "very Irish" persists only in the most remote areas of the West. I found it on an island that I would like to keep nameless, in the hope that I'll find it there still when I go back—a naive hope, no doubt. (When I first visited several years ago, the pub had a *ceili* night with dancing and song; now it has a Space Invaders video game.) Walking out to the lighthouse on my most recent visit, I stopped opposite a cottage where a farmer had made a field gate by propping up the rusting black door of a Morris Minor. He came out of the cottage for a chat. We made small talk about the commonage wall around the jointly held pasturage and about the fuchsia woven through the piers of his cottage gate, and then I asked him casually if there were ever any disputes on the island about stone walls, any hint of the petty divisions and small fiefdoms that often characterize Irish relations. "In the old days they had rows," he said. "That was because they had bad walls and people were always trespassing."

A bridge near Maancross in Connemara.

I tried to jog his memory a bit. The "ructions" and "holy wars" of the classic Irish boundary dispute were too wickedly ingenious to have slipped into oblivion. There was a farmer in the Burren, I said by way of example, who'd once built a wall not on the boundary line with a hated neighbor, but several feet back on his own land, so the neighbor had either to tether his animals or build a wall of his own to forestall crippling litigation for criminal trespass. (If the land in between the two walls went to waste, well, it probably hadn't been worth a box of matches to start with.) In another case, a farmer simply removed the half of a double wall that stood on his land, leaving his neighbor to deal with the perilously balanced remainder. My new acquaintance gave a brief, noncommittal laugh.

I told him next of a wall being used to commit "morder." (A sly, sideways-glancing stonemason had told me the story: "They killed a man. They didn't kill him fully like, but they done their best. They pitched him in over the wall and they dumped the wall on top of him. They just done it for divilment, like. They didn't like him. Sullivan, his name was. They broke his two legs and they broke his two hands.") Finally, there were disputes about animals crossing walls, sometimes abetted by their masters. In Connemara I stayed one night at a former estate house, now a hotel, and the proprietress explained her solid fences with a pointed aphorism: "If a goat gets in your garden, it belongs to nobody. If it gets in your pot, it belongs to everybody." A rural arbitrator I'd heard of had quit the business in frustration when one housewife brought suit because another woman's chickens were pecking the limewash off her walls.

*A farmer, Patrick Sharry, with a wall his grandfather
built in County Clare.*

Could all this parochial sound and fury, all this glorious rural entertainment, be lost in modern Ireland? Noll Gogarty, a barrister I had spoken with in Dublin, said yes: "The country people have stopped their litigation because it got so expensive and because they have other entertainments now. There were no cinemas then, and no television. There were old buffers who would bring action every year or two just for the day out in court, and they'd bring all their friends. But that's all gone now."

Standing on the island road, opposite the Morris Minor gate, in the sort of perpetual breeze that forces you to turn one ear to leeward in order to hear, I repeated a phrase this new acquaintance had just used. "In the old days?" I asked. "Aye," he said, intent on frustrating my search for modern instances of boundary dispute. Then as we parted, he told me his name, Paddy G———, and if my smile betrayed malicious delight, it was because I recognized the name and I knew in that instant that I had broken through a tissue of genial deceptions. This same Paddy G——— was, in fact, at that moment engaged in a nasty dispute with a neighbor just up the road, whom I had befriended on an earlier visit. According to my friend, Michael Joe O'Malley, the G——— brothers were practitioners of the black art of wall-knocking—creating gaps in walls to let their animals into somebody else's fields. It was "the best kind of theft" because the wind or the animals might have done the knocking, and there was little risk of ever having to compensate the victim for the lost hay.

But one day O'Malley, who is seventy years old, caught a G——— in the act and wound up rubbing his nose in cow dung. A solicitor from the mainland subsequently came after O'Malley for his "savage assault," threatening, in prose that quavered with moral indignation, to take him to court—unless he would pay cash damages of £100. Paddy G——— had gone out and bought an overcoat on the prospect. O'Malley admired the tailoring of it, but paid not a shilling. All this took place not "in the old days" but within the year.

To me this was lovely stuff, or anyway it was Ireland. Up the road, O'Malley welcomed me to rest my bones and broke out a bottle of whiskey. We talked about walls and about his boundary dispute with the G——— brothers. It was a conundrum: he felt chagrined because part of him is a pacifist, at least with regard to anyone other than his immediate neighbors, and yet he still relished something that the poet Patrick Kavanagh had once said—that "when he went into a bar and saw a man with a sticking plaster on his face and blood on his gansey, he knew he had reason to live." As entertainment, Space Invaders didn't stand a chance.

As ENTERTAINMENT, THE WALLS ALSO LOOM VERY large indeed in the eyes of a wholly different class of people—the members of the County Galway Hunt, better known as the Galway Blazers. For them, as for generations of the local gentry, leaping walls is what life is all about, on horseback, in the company of perhaps a hundred other riders, with

OVERLEAF

*On a road near Craughwell, Michael Dempsey
exercises the hounds of the County Galway Hunt.*

the hounds baying frantically just ahead. Even in the relatively broad fields of east Galway, a horse and rider with sufficient nerve and stamina might leap as many as a hundred field walls in a day, most of them 2- or 3-footers, but some up to 5 feet high.

One morning on a road outside Craughwell, I met Michael Dempsey, master of the hunt kennels, who was exercising sixty hounds. High on a bicycle, with his pack around him, Dempsey seemed to be riding on a frantic tide of hound, every animal desperate for attention and yet shamefaced when caught in some trivial incivility: "Badger, get back here! Brigid, get over here when you're told!" They assembled around him by a wall in a field, and at his command they went over in a wave, like a dam bursting. Springing, leaping, scrambling like maniacs as loose stones fell thunking behind them, the hounds were in ecstasy. "I suppose it's not so nice for the fox," Dempsey reflected.

Ah, but the fox loves the walls, too, he concluded. "He'll get up and run for fifty or a hundred yards right on top of the wall and then make a big leap as far as he can into the woods, and the hounds lose the scent. Or he'll drop down close to the wall, just jinker the bottom of the wall, and the hounds go over. The fox is just laughing at them, and that's what he does most of the time."

That evening, Dempsey sent me on to see three members of the hunt putting on a private wall-jumping exhibition for their own pleasure and for twenty black-eyed cattle lined up along a wall, like punters at the rail, to watch. The cattle were the most curious and attentive I have ever seen. Bovine eyes followed each rider, heads swinging in unison from the start and up for the leap, then back to the

*For members of the County Galway Hunt, leaping
walls is the stuff of life. Says the master of the hounds:
"I suppose it's not so nice for the fox."*

start. Even to them the jumping must have seemed beautiful, with the three riders all done up in boots, brown hunting jackets, and dark caps. We were on a hilltop, and the landscape was also lovely: rolling green hills under the aluminum light of the evening sun, a lake nearby, Galway Bay in the distance. After the workout, the riders turned and headed down to the road at a trot. They went down not through the open fields, but along a wall, and they continued leaping all the way down, for the lark of it.

The three of them went back and forth across the wall, and their paths wove together like the ribbons of dancers circling a maypole. It was a glorious scene, with the huffing of the horses, the metallic clink of horseshoes on limestone, the audible trampling of the grass, the kicking up of loose dirt. One emotion I had never connected with Irish walls was pure joy, but I felt at that moment as if the whole wall-ribbed countryside were swelling up in celebration.

ARAN

I F WALLS ARE
the spine and the ribs of the Irish landscape,
then it makes sense that so many of them are
built of limestone—an amalgam of bones,
shells, and teeth from the inhabitants of a
tropical sea that covered Ireland more than
270 million years ago. It must have been an
abundant sea, to judge only by the monuments of compacted bone that it left behind.

Limestone lies under about half of Ireland's
total area, but it makes its most spectacular

appearance in the Aran Islands. There, at the mouth of Galway Bay, the rock emerges from below the waterline on the landward side, forms the gradually ascending rock terraces of the three islands, and finally fronts the Atlantic with cliffs as much as 400 feet in height. The limestone, intercut with layers of shale, runs from the bare pavements of the clifftops to an unknown depth under the seabed. In the nearby Burren, of which the islands are an extension, the limestone is 3,000 feet deep. Limestone has made the three islands, Inisheer, Inishmaan, and Inishmore, a world not just of stones, but of walls, in a quantity—a *density*—found nowhere else in Ireland. Here the skeleton of the earth comes to the surface, and people somehow thrive on it.

One afternoon on Inisheer, the smallest of the islands, I climbed up to an old hill fort encircling the ruins of a sixteenth-century castle. The sun blazed on a field of man-made earth, supporting daisies and buttercups. Two choughs, a type of red-beaked crow, skimmed acrobatically along the edge of the cashel wall. The scene beyond was quintessentially Irish. Kevin Danaher had told me that there were 240,000 miles of walls in Ireland, but if he had said there were enough walls to reach from Ballyvaughan to Jupiter, and if he had added that he was talking only about the walls on Inisheer, I might have believed him. "Nothing only walls as far as the eye can see," a Clare man had promised, correctly. That was Inisheer, an island of ovals, trapezoids, paisley squiggles of land, like a map of a whole nation, with walls representing every quirky parish border.

Inisheer was special not just because of the number of walls, but because the walls clearly still retain some of their ancient status as a daily concern among the islanders. Where modern farmers on the mainland routinely bulldoze walls to "knock together" an inefficient clutch of small fields, the islanders are still throwing up walls and dividing land. "Some of our parks are very large," a farmer told me, eyeing a half-acre patch as if it were Kansas.

The walls were once a necessity for manufacturing fields. Except in the deep vertical fissures, called "grikes," nothing grew on the pavements of limestone that formed the original surface of the three islands. The land had to be made, and the size of the modern fields reflects the difficulty of their creation. A farmer working with a horse or donkey could reasonably expect to cover no more than a quarter-acre with the makings of dirt in a single winter. So-called gardens of this size thus predominate (anything larger is known as a "park," from the Irish word for field). In making a "garden," the farmer first assembled the litter of blocky stones into a wall. If the land contained grikes, he scooped out their rich black contents—the only authentic soil to go into the mix—and replaced them with loose stones. Then came basket after basket of sand, seaweed, and manure. The walls held back the winds while this rough blend moldered into arable earth. "They improved the place great, all right," a farmer told me.

In the process, the people of Aran put their mark on the island, and the island on them. The walls created places, and the map of these places seems to have imprinted itself on the minds of the people. A farmer might own twenty-five or thirty fields, and there might be thousands of fields

*Granite boulders left behind by the receding glaciers
stand out here and there amid the dark limestone of the
Aran Islands.*

on the island, but each acquired its own name: The Crag of the Ghosts, The Field of the Heads. Tim Robinson, an artist who lived on Inishmore for ten years and minutely mapped all three islands, has written of the walls as a "web of stone" that catches and embodies the spirit of the people: "As I write I think of details far beyond the powers of resolution of this map—a little field called *An Dug,* the dock, because it is shaped like Galway harbour, another called Dingle because its soil came from Kerry as ballast in boats coming for kelp, a third called *Moinin an Damhsa,* the little meadow of the dancing, because someone saw the fairies dancing there. . . ."

Within each field, the walls still reveal, by their style and skillfulness, the character of their builders. A granite boulder set high up in a wall as an act of exuberant boastfulness testifies to the great strength of the brothers, now long dead, who put it there. A wall thrown up teeter-totter style, more light and air than rock, commemorates the haste of its builder, for the time being.

"Some men can tell by looking at a wall who built it," one of the island schoolteachers told me, "just as the women can tell by looking at a jumper who stitched it."

One evening at sunset, I walked out on the uninhabited west end of Inisheer, among single walls and double walls, walls where the rocks were wedged in at an angle like books leaning on a shelf, and walls where horizontal stones seemed to be stitched in place with a cross-weave of verticals. It was a Godforsaken spot to be a farmer, but the walls revealed a delight in the nature of the stone, an unearthly patience with the land, an almost artistic satisfaction in the slow shaping of this world. At

Small miracles of balance keep a wall upright
on Inisheer.

OVERLEAF
Sunset on Inishmore.

dusk, when the air grew dark, the stones seemed to hold on briefly to the light of day, and the whole island became an eerie, phosphorescent maze of walls, without trees or shrubs or buildings to mar the effect. Minos might have lived here.

I F THE ARAN LANDSCAPE SOMETIMES SEEMS EERIE IN its starkness, limestone is an important reason. In one sense, limestone is very regular—indeed, almost geometrical. Cut vertically by the grikes and horizontally by the layering of the sedimentary deposits that formed it, it breaks naturally into rough blocks well suited to construction. They look like loaves of bread with fissured crusts. But limestone is strange stuff.

To begin with, limestone is soluble in mild acids. Long rains have thus been able to mold it, and they have had the odd effect of making it smooth in some places and jagged in others. The rainwater running down a wall seems to soften the bread-crust fissures. The stones become living things. You sense this in the least likely places. Dun Aengus, on Inishmore, for instance, is one of the most ferociously defended points in all Europe; it sits atop a cliff 280 feet above the Atlantic. But the main wall, 18 feet high and 13 feet thick, gently follows the contours of the land, rising and falling; the millions of stones seem to have grown together so that they sag and bulge and undulate as one

On the ramparts of Dun Aengus, Inishmore.

organism. Even the rain-worn pavements of the island have a kind of softness, where they remain exposed. Summer visitors to the islands use them as ready-made beds for sunbathing.

But the rain has also cut the deep grikes down through the pavement, and it has pocked the surface in places with small potholes. Around each of these holes, the dissolved limestone has been redeposited in a sharp corona. Broken out of the pavement and fitted into a wall, stones with these features look like eye sockets, pelvic bones, vertebrae, bits of skulls. At Dun Aengus, the redeposited limestone forms sharp ridges on the tops of blocks set upright in the ground. A 30-foot-wide band of these uprights, called *chevaux de frise,* stands as a belly-ripping defense against attackers on horseback or on foot. No one knows who defended the Aran forts, or who attacked them. But limestone is porous; it would have soaked up the blood of both sides.

THE ISLAND CULTURE, WHICH IS SO KEENLY ATTUNED to the spirit of place, is oddly indifferent to matters of history. This has presented an awkward hindrance to those who have made the islanders a symbol of Celtic virtue and independence in an adverse world. No one really knows if their forebears were Greeks, as legend has it, or Englishmen, as iconoclasts sometimes argue, or, after all, Celts. People have lived on the Aran Islands since as

Tethered to a wall, a donkey awaits its burden.
Donkeys roam the lanes of the island at night,
often making mischief.

OVERLEAF
A farmer cinches together sheaves of grain, to be used
for feed and roof thatching.

early as 1600 B.C., the date of the first known archeological site. The islands may have served as a last refuge for early cultures driven across Ireland by newcomers. They are also known to have been a retreat for saints, and a hiding place for outlawed priests and Irish revolutionaries.

Roughly 1,500 people live there now. They have television sets to relieve the boredom of the long winters (a woman on Inishmore has named her dog Pam, after a character on the television show "Dallas"), as well as other modern conveniences. The men wear running shoes with Velcro snaps, instead of the traditional rawhide pampooties. On Inishmaan, the most traditional of the islands, the women knit thoroughly untraditional sweaters for sale on Madison Avenue and in Tokyo. But the limestone persists, and, especially on Inishmaan, it shapes a world of Biblical orderliness and ferocity.

The orderliness shows up in small things. All over the island, in September, farmers cut rye and cinch it into yellow sheaves to dry against a wall. Here and there, a sheaf swings in a golden blur over a thresher's head to separate, on the limestone pavement, into grain for feed and straw for thatch. (Sometimes the islanders save a sprig of grain to set in the peak of a thatched roof, like a feather in a cap.) In another field, a great rampart of hay is heaped over a wall to dry, and a donkey waits to haul it in for winter storage. The donkey's saddle is an antique device of tarred canvas and wooden yoke, with a mat of straw stuffed underneath as a saddle blanket. Fully loaded, the donkey will disappear under its burden—a moving, quadruped haycock. (The donkeys are everywhere on the island, and sometimes wander free when they are not at work. They are "great rogues," a farmer assured me, and

Bringing in the hay on Inishmaan.

will find a gap and furtively knock it down in the night, nosing out one stone at a time so as not to alert the dogs. There is hell to pay for the lost potatoes or cabbages when this happens, so the gaps are customarily braided with a thorn bush for protection.) The islanders convey a reassuring sense of being busy about the earth even in their most jarringly modern moments. One day on Inishmaan, I had to step aside for a motor scooter roaring up a narrow lane. A teenage boy stood on the pedals and steered. His father sat behind with a huge ram stretched in blind terror across his lap.

Elsewhere on the island, an old-fashioned farmer has set cow pats on a wall to dry. There is no turf on any of the islands, and while his neighbors mostly import gas or coal, he has a shed full of manure to burn as winter fuel. (In the past, the islanders imported turf from Connemara. To pay for it, they exported lime, which they manufactured by stacking layers of turf and limestone in a kiln, and burning the rock.) There is little waste in the island's traditional husbandry of its meager resources. Even a waterlogged patch of lowland is walled in to make a "sally garden," where so-called sally rods are grown. Though not much used now, the leafy willow rods milling about in the breeze there are the raw material for baskets and lobster pots.

The walls are merely the framework for all these agricultural doings. They shape the countryside. No one can really say whether they shape the character of the people as well; but I am inclined to think that when people stay in a place long enough, the land enters their souls. If the islanders have been in Aran for more than 3,500 years—roughly 165 generations—one might well expect wall-

A farmer—Peter Conneely of West Village,
Inishmaan—opens a gap to let livestock into a field.

building to have coded itself into their genes. The islanders themselves are far too reserved to talk about such things. But a woman who now lives on the mainland told me about a characteristic void in her perception of the world: on a trip to France once, she did not know what to look at when a friend pointed out landscape after landscape dominated by lovely trees. "I hate the *smell* of trees," she added, with some embarrassment.

The familiarity with stones begins in childhood. The same woman, now in her early thirties, remembered that stones were her first toys. Bits of rock served as make-believe cattle, sheep, and chickens. She made fields for them, enclosed with 6-inch-high walls, and took down a miniature gap when the limestone animals wanted to go in or out.

This intimacy persists into old age. A woman who lived on Inishmore for ten years (and was thus a "blow-in," an outsider) recalled sheltering behind a wall in a rainstorm one day. An elderly islander of her acquaintance joined her there. The rain picked up, and droplets were coming through the wall. As the old man complained to her about how he had become crippled in his dotage and would never walk again, the woman noticed that he was tucking small stones into the gaps in the wall, to improve the shelter. It became quite cozy. Then the weather broke, and the old man hopped onto his bicycle and pedaled off.

The walls have served even in death. On Inishmaan, the most important wall is the boundary splitting the island into two townlands, and the taboo against altering it in any way remains strong. It is

Mrs. Kate Cooke, 88, of Bungowla, a village on the western tip of Inishmore.

a political divide, with separate rights and responsibilities on each side. (The strand where the wall ends is known as the Shore of the Quarrels because, without the clear divide, disputes about owner-ship of the seaweed that washed up there were common.) But the boundary wall was also the burial place for unbaptized children, whose souls, according to Catholic doctrine, went not to heaven or hell, but to limbo. Was the wall chosen as a burial place to disperse the responsibility for these unset-tled souls? Or to reduce the likelihood of haunting (that is, by providing them with the option of haunting the *other* townland)? Or did the wall become a burial place simply because ground deep enough for grave-digging was scarce?

No one remembers now, and speculations by outsiders are risky. A clever priest who was a new-comer to the Aran Islands once employed the walls in a sermon. He urged each of the islanders to become a great wall of faith, not *claí fidín,* a wall of little bits. This made perfect sense to him. But to the islanders, the *claí fidín* was the hardest to build and the most prized, composed of densely packed bits of rock at the bottom between upright "mother stones." Such a wall, with the larger stones set improbably on top, spoke of the almost magical skill of the builder. The sermon flopped.

The symbolic standing of the Aran Islanders and their Irish-speaking culture has made them the subject of endless scrutiny and foolishness on the part of outsiders. Only one investigator, though, a sociologist who visited in the 1960s, seems to have incurred their wrath. He did not dwell on their independence or on their ability to make a life from the rugged endowment of limestone and sea, but

*Colm Mor Faherty of Inishmaan remembers when
courting couples and eavesdroppers alike hid themselves
behind the island walls.*

on their isolation. On these islands, the neighbors are neighbors for life, and they constitute one's world to a degree that must be as intimidating as it is reassuring. Since an ill-chosen or foolish word to a neighbor can have lifelong repercussions, human intimacy is rare. Instead, the sociologist wrote about the "ubiquity of jealousy and envy," about young men spying on people from behind walls in order to report their misbehavior, about intense pressures to conformity, about a profound fear of uncovered flesh (bathing was almost nonexistent and fishermen often drowned because they never learned to swim), and about the cold and withdrawn character of the islanders' married life. The people had indeed become *claí fidín,* but they had walled themselves up against each other.

The sociologist's book did not sell in Ireland, partly because it painted an extreme and unduly harsh picture, but also because it told some hard truths about a national symbol. It is worth mentioning here because of the obvious parallel between the isolation of the lives the sociologist depicted and the islanders' ceaseless walling up of their landscape. It seems too labored to suggest that the social world and the landscape are necessarily bound up together, or that one is cause and the other reflection. But surely the parallel isn't just coincidence. One possibility, and one I like, is that, for the islanders, the building of the walls became a distraction from the isolation of their lives—a consolation, even. If they were intimate with anything, it was the limestone. In handling it, in piling one stone lovingly on top of another, in working out the delicate problems of balance, strength, and beauty, perhaps a builder could for once lose himself in the endless network of walls.

ONE EVENING ON INISHEER, I VISITED THOMAS Conneely, a publican, who had recently built a wall of huge stones and who was reportedly given to spending half a day out on the back of the island contemplating the suitability of a particular stone. He was strong and straight-backed, and he spoke with a sort of diffident lockjaw, audibly sucking in his breath at the end of a phrase as if he had learned to speak partly among the donkeys that wander the island's lanes. First in Irish, then in English, he recited the basic rule of wall-building for me: "One stone on two and two stones on one." I found this cryptic, so he demonstrated with several packs of cigarettes.

"Walls are more important than people," he declared, as he constructed a wall between us on the bar. A row of packs set end-to-end formed the first course. The second course went in, each pack bridging two packs below it and, when the third course was added, supporting two packs above. A solid sort of wall. "You see people everywhere in the world, and they're more or less the same." But every wall had its special character and function, like the one he'd just built to prevent the winter tides from washing away the field in front of his house, or like the one he was working on at the back of the island to make a field secure against rabbits, which are the bane of agriculture on the islands.

"The stones are nice," he concluded. "They don't insult you."

ACKNOWLEDGMENTS

The authors wish to thank Robert Feldman
for his enthusiastic help in selecting the pictures
for this book. They also thank the Irish Tourist
Board, Aer Lingus, *Geo* magazine, and the
many others who generously cooperated with
this project.

DESIGN

J. C. Suarès
Kathleen Gates
Steve Neumann
Andrea Perrine

PRODUCTION

Katherine van Kessel

Composed in Bembo by Arkotype Inc.,
New York, New York
Printed and bound by
Toppan Printing Company, Ltd.,
Tokyo, Japan